to whom it may concern

a collection of poetry and prose

samantha tellez

samantha tellez

ISBN: 978-1-7975-9246-6

to whom it may concern

to myself.

it was only upon selecting which pieces of the hundreds I have written would make it into this book that I came to the realization that I have never written a poem to myself. while it is true that without my many muses these works would not exist, it is also true that they would have never found their way onto paper without my hand. "to whom it may concern" would not be a reality without the service of my mind, body, and soul. but, like too many others-especially women-I have grown accustomed to denying myself credit and as a result, at times, I feel that I am not deserving of it. so much so, that I feel a need to write an entire paragraph justifying my dedication. so, this is my poem. all of it.

samantha tellez

to whom it may concern

table of contents

samantha tellez

to whom it may concern

every person I've encountered on this journey deserves endless appreciation for helping me get here. I owe more 'thank you's than I could probably ever give. especially to Raquel, Abelardo, Sofia and Amy Tellez. to Joan Vick. to Jennifer Watson, Jennifer John, Dale McCarthy, Aimee Blochberger, Kaj Miller and Melissa Hinton. to Stacey Graham, Mark Durante and Adam Udell. to Payton Groff, Claire Croft, and Ashleigh Mckenna. and to every lover that has been a muse to me, thank you. you have all made me a better writer, but above all, a better person. thank you so much.

and to you, dear reader, for allowing this book to concern you:

I thank you.

samantha tellez

to whom it may concern

LEARNING

samantha tellez

slowly but surely,
I am learning that
me not being to you,
what you are to me,
is a beginning
and not an end.
even if now,
we are nothing,
we have the potential
to be something.
and how beautiful it would be
for us to reach our full.

to whom it may concern

I want to know you.
not just your name, but the reason why your mother chose it and if
you prefer the shortened version of it.

I want to know you.
not just your favorite color, but why that shade of blue trumps all the
others and why it looks so much like her eyes.

I want to know you.
not just your favorite quote, but why it speaks to you and what it
means to you.

I want to know you.
not just your family, but where they came from and why you don't
speak to your dad's side of it.

I want to know you.
not just your heart, but what it beats for and if there's any room for
me in it.

samantha tellez

sometimes I cannot believe
the simplicity of our origin,
knowing the complexity of our now.

to whom it may concern

simply because we were
good to each other
does not mean that we were
good for each other.
I must keep that in my mind,
and not keep you in my heart.

and I think the hardest part to accept
is that you took advantage of me.
it does not matter that I let you,
you did not have to.

to whom it may concern

is it a sin to say
that I miss you,
but that I am also
so glad that you didn't stay?

I'm a fool enough
to still long for your touch
but I am wise enough
to not ask for it.

samantha tellez

loving someone who does not *not* love you
but loves someone else more than they love you,
is worse than loving someone who does not love you.

to whom it may concern

from time to time I hear your name,
and it sounds a lot like my childhood.
something that I still admire,
but have moved past from as I should.

it's been ages,
of that, I am well aware.
and although it doesn't seem like it,
I'm beginning not to care.

long ago you gave me the key,
but it no longer fits.
and it's starting to seem like I'm over you,
but just not over it.

samantha tellez

you think you love me,
but I know I love you.
now, I don't know
what you feel,
but what I do know is that
if there's hesitation, it can't be real.

a man who loves your body
but not your heart,
not your mind,
not your soul,
does not love you.
remember that,
before you give him
your all.

samantha tellez

we could have been
so beautiful,
but you never
saw me as such.
I always was,
we just never were.

to whom it may concern

you are the morning after.

the pang of regret that only ever seems to hit after 6 a.m.
you are what I know I shouldn't have done,
but did anyway.

the sense of guilt that doesn't go away until it knows it has left its mark.
you are what I never needed,
but wanted anyway.

the reminder I wish I could ignore.
you are what I should have thought twice about,
but didn't think once about.

you are the morning after.

samantha tellez

maybe I still love you despite how terribly you treated me because I know how good you could treat me.

despite how ill you spoke of me because I know how sweet your words once were.

and despite how bad we were because I know how good we could be.

to whom it may concern

years have gone by and it's no longer
"I miss you", nor is it, "I need to move on" but, "I should have".

I should have loved you more. I should have never let you go. I should have treated you better. I should have never let you down. I should have never given you a reason to leave. I should have given you more reasons to stay.

perhaps tomorrow, it will be "I should have left sooner".

samantha tellez

you taught me so much
and I know I should be grateful,
but it's things I wish
I never knew.

to whom it may concern

I can't even breathe the same
let alone ever be.
you are entirely to blame
and it's taken me too damn long to see.

it never was,
and never will be my fault.
I am the way I am
because of you and your assault.

he took advantage.
he is a user.
he did the damage.
he is an abuser.

we were broken into,
but we are not broken.
you are still you.
so please, let your voice be spoken.

say it with me,
"I didn't deserve it"
say it with me,
"I didn't deserve it one bit".

samantha tellez

you are heartbroken,
but you are not broken.
he took a piece of you
that you may never have again,
but you are not split in two.
there is so much more to you
than what he took.

to whom it may concern

I haven't forgotten your name,
but it's no longer the only one I know.
I haven't forgotten your face,
but it's no longer the only one I see.
I haven't forgotten your voice,
but it's no longer the only one I hear.
I haven't forgotten you,
but you're no longer the only one.

samantha tellez

if he loved you,
he would show it.
if he loved you,
you would know it.
love is not a maybe thing.
when you are loving,
and being loved in return,
there will be no question.

to whom it may concern

if you find yourself
loving him more
than you love yourself,
take a step back.

remember that no man
can love you so much
that it will replace
the love for you that you lack.

samantha tellez

perhaps we were
not meant to be,
but meant to meet.

to whom it may concern

when the tides roll much too high,
I think of us and wonder why
we always thought we were a little too much.

          when the color of the leaves fail to change,
                    I think of us and wonder why
              we couldn't accept ourselves as we were.

when the flowers cease to bloom,
I think of us and wonder why
we never thought that we could still be something beautiful.

          when the snow hardly even leaves a coat of frost,
                I think of us and wonder why
          we ever thought we had to leave a mark on the world.

samantha tellez

I'm only kidding myself
when I say I'm afraid of forgetting you.
it's not that I'm not,
but that we both know
you gave me too much to ever forget.

to whom it may concern

black jeans,
button-down,
you're wearing a smile
but I know you'll only give me a frown.

leather jacket,
black shoes,
life of the party
but I know you're bad news.

sly smile,
green eyes,
looking for a little fun
but I know you're just like the other guys.

samantha tellez

you were everything.
I was nothing.
and now you're just something,
and I'm rightfully everything.

to whom it may concern

you know everything,
I don't know much.
but there is one thing
that I know, and you don't.

I know how to love
and how to truly care.
if you are willing,
this is something I could share.

you know more than I do
when it comes to everything else.
but this is the one thing
that to be known, first must be felt.

samantha tellez

I learned to live with the intervals of time
and that the good moments will always pass.
but the moment our lips pressed together,
I couldn't help but wonder why
the greatest moments in life never last.

to whom it may concern

upon reflection
of every heart I have ever
chased after
and every soul I have ever
longed for
I see one parallel.
it is not that
they are all hazel-eyed
or that
they all carry a haughty smile,
but that not one of them
chased after my heart
or longed for my soul.

oh, but every last one of them
wrestled for my body.

like a trophy
they could display on a shelf
above their bed
amongst the others they've won
-but never earned-
along the way.

samantha tellez

maybe the ability to see someone
the way in which they were brought into this world
with blurry vision
and incapable of distinguishing them from the others,
despite bearing no resemblance,
comes from experience with this sort of thing.

if such is the case, I wish to forever remain
inexperienced.

to whom it may concern

she won't love you
like I did,
but all that matters
is that she does.

samantha tellez

you say you love the snow, but hate the cold. and I now understand that you can love the gift, but not the giver. and I now understand that though you loved what I gave you, you never loved me.

to whom it may concern

dear future self,
I hope you learn
that the true meaning of love
is to be loved in return.

I hope you learn
that when it comes to love
you may have to wait your turn.

I hope you learn
that with love
you will smile, but you will yearn.

dear future self,
if you're reading this
ten years down the road
I hope you have learned
that love is a spark
and you mustn't let it burn.

samantha tellez

it's hard to see the girls who came before me and not dwell on the similarities or lack thereof. I see the blonde you went to high school with whose cute smile is composed of lips much thinner than mine. did they feel better on yours than my full ones do? I obsess over the brunette I know was your first love, even though you refuse to call her that, and how much her figure truly represents an hourglass. did the time you spent nuzzled in her curves seem to go by faster with her than it does with me? I haven't stopped thinking about that girl you introduced me to at that party in your basement and those gorgeous, seemingly endless locks. is she the reason why you say you love my long hair so much? I wish I could forget your coworker with the damn near invisible waist. when you grab mine as tightly as you do, I can't help but wonder if you are trying to squeeze it down to resemble her's. and I think of that sweet girl who grew up on the same avenue as you who embodies natural beauty in every sense of the phrase and wonder if my bright yellow nail polish or red lipstick secretly turns you off.

why is it so hard for me to remember that just like you once chose them, you also chose me?

it takes strength
to realize that
he's not a bad person
for not being able
to give you the love
you so deserve.

samantha tellez

how liberating it is
to accept that
you giving someone
all of your heart
doesn't earn you
a single piece of theirs.

to whom it may concern

LEAVING

samantha tellez

you're leaving me,
but that doesn't mean
that I have to leave me, too.
like when you loved me,
even though I didn't.

to whom it may concern

I am fearful
that if I continue
to bend for you
in every way
you demand,
I will break.

"I'll miss you" you say as you put your key in the ignition and turn to face me through your rolled down window. I wonder how much truth that statement can hold if you've already made up your mind on leaving. I do not doubt that you'll miss the familiarity that I carry with me, like a spritz of perfume I put on every day that you only ever take note of if it's absent. I do not doubt that you'll miss the comfort I granted you, like your childhood bed that you no longer fit in, but could never truly grow out of. I do not doubt that you'll miss the warmth of my skin against yours, like dampened fingertips that stick to sand but never get stuck. I do not doubt that you'll miss the home I built for us, deep within ourselves with the only key being the other.

"I'll miss you, too" I say as I take a step back and watch you drive away, knowing that only one of us made a confession.

to whom it may concern

I gave you my all
immediately.
so that when you decide
on which piece of me to take,
it'll sting a little less.

samantha tellez

you got what you wanted,
but you are what I wanted.
you have a piece of me,
I have none of you.

to whom it may concern

like when an eraser
rubs against a piece of paper
to rid of words,

there will always be a mark.

I cannot erase you
without leaving
an obvious trace of you.

samantha tellez

it's been a year now
and I still haven't forgotten
the way you turned my heart inside out
and turned me bitter and rotten.

darling, it's been a year now
and I still can't forget
how our beautiful love
came to a sudden, abrupt end.

to whom it may concern

I wish I had met you sooner.
maybe that way,
we could have been more
than what we were.

1) *I still have your mother's phone number.*
2) *you took advantage of me. you know it, I know it. although I acted like I was okay with it, I wasn't. I never was. and I don't think I ever will be.*
3) *I lied when I said us seeing other people was a good idea. that was the only time I ever lied to you.*
4) *I'd come back to you in a heartbeat if you asked me to.*
5) *our song is still my favorite song.*
6) *I always knew she was more than "just a friend".*
7) *I haven't deleted our pictures together.*
8) *you didn't lose your spare keys, they're still at my mom's place.*
9) *it wasn't okay for you to leave me like that, even if I said it was.*
10) *I really meant it when I said I want you to be happy.*
11) *sometimes I worry that I will never get over you.*
12) *I still play your voicemails.*
13) *you gave love a new meaning.*
14) *I loved you. I always have and something tells me that I always will. and I have tried time after time to show you, but it seems as if you've gone blind.*

- *14 things I'll never tell you (although I probably should)*

to whom it may concern

March was leaving my fingertips
and soon enough, so were you.
when April came around,
it's a shame that you didn't, too.

samantha tellez

I feel your absence every day,
but today especially.
it's like living in Seattle.
it always rains,
I'm used to it.
but today,
I left my umbrella in the car.

to whom it may concern

hating you is bad, but loving you is worse.

samantha tellez

you are the sun.
no longer because you're beautiful,
but because you burn.

you are the ocean.
no longer because you're serene,
but because you drown me.

you are the snow.
no longer because you're soft,
but because you're cold.

you are the rain.
no longer because you're soothing,
but because you never stop.

to whom it may concern

I loved you,
the minute I saw you.
you loved me,
the minute I left you.

samantha tellez

to the boy who broke my heart,
I'll have you know
that although just barely
my heart survived your mighty blow.

to the boy who broke my heart,
even though it's hardly true
you cannot call me a liar
for saying that I'm over you.

to the boy who broke my heart,
through all the pain you had me endure
thank you for showing me
that you were never worth fighting for.

to whom it may concern

but I still vividly remember
the love we had in the midst of September
and the memories made
in October
and the love made
in November
and the mess made
in mid-December
and the love lost
somewhere in-between.

samantha tellez

your lips were an ink pen,
and mine a sheet of paper.
now that you're gone,
I can't write anymore.

to whom it may concern

tomorrow was never a promise,
and neither were you;
you left once the clock struck 12,
as if it was your cue.

the minute you left,
I fancied the thought that you wanted to stay;
but I was never in your plans,
and you went astray.

yesterday you were mine,
today you're merely a thought;
this love was a war,
but you never fought.

samantha tellez

last week
I was your precious love.
this week
I am your previous love.

-   typo

you think you're over it, you always do. but then, you see them. and their eyes mirror everything you once had. their lips speak to you without parting, asking you if you remember the last time they met with yours. their hands touch you without leaving their sides while they have you feel everything you haven't felt since they left your side. their eyebrows will furrow together to ask if you remember the last time you were that close. and their smile will curve up as if they mean to remind you of the direction you were going before it all went down. and you think you're over it, you always do. but then, you see them.

samantha tellez

and to this day,
I don't know whether
you were
one of the best things,
or
one of the worst things
that has ever happened to me.

to whom it may concern

my heart has been
preparing to love you
for the past sixteen years
that it's been beating.

it's such a shame
that the day I learned to love you,
your heart and all its feelings
went fleeting.

you see, baby,
the truth is,
my heart has been trying to love you
since the day of our meeting.

samantha tellez

I gave you pieces of me
that I cannot take back.
you do not love me anymore;
you only loved me for what I now lack.

I wish you could give it back,
or take me back.
you are what I love,
and you are what I lack.

to whom it may concern

you found me
when I was in the midst
of finding myself.
so let there be no doubt that
when I lost myself,
it's because I lost you.

samantha tellez

when our eyes lock,
I see everything
that I swore I forgot.

I see the love
that we once said
was sent from above.

agonizing reminders of everything we did,
everything we didn't do,
and all that lies in-between.

flashbacks of what was,
what always will be
and of course, everything that never was.

to whom it may concern

and your name will forever
poison the air of my thoughts,
and form a lump in my throat.
you'll make it hard to breathe,
and make me wonder,
where I went wrong,
and where I went right.
why I let you go,
and why you didn't
put up more of a fight.

samantha tellez

you treated my body
like an overnight hotel stay.

you never failed to let it be known
that I was just a rest stop on your way.

there was nothing I could do or say
to keep you another day.

and when you left, you left a mess of me,
but it was okay.

isn't it someone else's job
to look after me anyway?

and every now and again,
I hear a voice inside of my head
telling me that I should have never
let what we had end.

believe me,
I never dared to wish you away
but when it came to your feelings
I didn't have a say.

part of me is well aware
that I may still have a chance
and although you are all I ever wanted
I can't change the fact that you don't care.

and every now and again,
I pray to God for another chance
but perhaps it's best
that I let what we had end.

samantha tellez

ten years will go by and I'll still get chills when I hear your name.

ten years will go by and your voice will remain a lullaby to me when
I'm going insane.

ten years will go by and I won't forget the day you entered my life,
even when I wish you never came.

to whom it may concern

we met on the first Friday of the month at a local cafe.
you ordered a chai latte.
I ordered a cup of chamomile tea.
and things were never quite the same since that day.

we talked more than we drank;
I remember our cups were still half empty.
you made me laugh, and I made you smile.
who would've thought, you'd be the death of me.

we loved more than we intended to.
and since that afternoon, something grew in me that never went away.
you gave me something no one else could,
and it's such a shame that you didn't stay.

samantha tellez

the words you called me became my name tag.
I defined myself by your definition of me.
and so,
the way you saw me,
became the way I saw myself.
the way you spoke to me,
became the way I spoke to myself.
the way you loved me,
became the way I loved myself.
and so,
one day,
I didn't either.

it's as if your voice is telling me who I am,
and I am a slave to your words.
every word that escapes your lips comes to life
and molds me into a new person.

your voice writes me austere orders
that I have no choice but to follow.
and to be fair,
I'm tired of following the rules.

samantha tellez

last night,
I got asked to dance, but I declined.
I said, "I have a boyfriend"
but he didn't know,
that my boyfriend hasn't kissed me in over a month.

two nights ago,
my mom asked me why you didn't accompany me to her place.
I said, "he's been really busy"
but she didn't know
that you have been too busy
to even speak to me for the past eight days.

three nights ago,
my best friend asked
if we, the four of us, could go on a double date this weekend.
I said, "we'll see"
but she didn't know
that I can't even remember
the last time that we, the two of us, went on a date.

four nights ago,
your sister asked how we were.
I said "I'm fine" and "he's great"
but I think she knew,
that I could only speak for myself.

five nights ago,
I asked myself
"how much longer are you going to keep this up for?"
before I completely lose it,
and before I completely lose you.

- five nights, one doubt

to whom it may concern

but I'll be here,
if you change your mind.
or when you realize that
you were always better off being mine.

samantha tellez

what he thinks
does not matter,
neither does what he says.
what does matter
is what he does.
and if he is not fighting for you,
if he is not fighting for your love,
why are you?

to whom it may concern

our time together was sand slipping through our hands,
we could only hold on for so long.
but you made every second worth it,
you were my sweet summer song.

we were the sun and the sea;
two completely different things.
I called you my summer love,
you called me your summer fling.

samantha tellez

*he says he wants to "keep you around". like a tool you bought for a home
renovation project. you aren't sure if you'll ever use it again but hell, for
the amount of work you went through to get your hands on it, it better
be good for another use. or like a spice you have in the corner of the
highest shelf in your kitchen just because a recipe you made years ago
called for it. you always say you want to try it again because you loved it
at one point. or like a gown you have had collecting dust in your closet
for as long as you can remember. you don't want to admit it, but you
have a sentimental attachment to it, so it'll stay. or like a gift you
received from an ex-lover six Christmases ago. you simply don't have the
heart to get rid of it, even though deep down, you know you should.*

I feel like I am simply an unchecked box on your to-do list, only as significant as washing your whites or picking up your prescription from the CVS on your way home from work. at my best, I am something you must get done and you let out a sigh of relief the minute you realize you don't have to give me another thought. you can cross me off. you don't have to worry about me for another few weeks, or if I'm lucky, you'll be out running errands sometime soon and happen to think of me. if such is the case, you are more than welcome to get me out of the way, just while you're at it.

samantha tellez

it's funny to compare
the number of words
we've spoken to each other
in the past few weeks
to the number of words
I've written about you since.

to whom it may concern

LIVING

samantha tellez

you are a flower,
and he may be the sun.
but, you need water, too.
he alone
cannot give you life.
the biggest mistake
you can make is
believe that a man
in solitude
will help you grow.

to whom it may concern

the nape of my neck
is sprouting flowers
from the seeds
that you planted
with your lips
and watered
with your tongue.
your kiss
brought life to me.
don't you dare say,
"it was just a kiss"

samantha tellez

all my life
I've been in search of
something worth living for.
I found you,
but now I fear
you are all I live for.
you are not something.
you are everything.

to whom it may concern

you go back and forth
between loving me
and hating me.
I don't want to live like this
but at least
you always come
back to me.

samantha tellez

you played games
with me
without
ever telling me
the rules.

to whom it may concern

and I still hope you're happy, even though you made me the opposite.

samantha tellez

you're like my great aunt's house
miles north of Chicago.
a place I've only stayed at
for numbered moments,
yet the very place
I feel most at home in.
far enough from the chaos
to be sound,
yet close enough
that I never knew what boredom was.
new enough that I still
have a twinkle in my eye
when I think of this place
yet, familiar enough,
that I feel I could drop in at any moment
even if you never invite me in.

to whom it may concern

I think the world could be
a much more beautiful place
if we all trusted that love
existed in every passing face.

I know we, as humans,
have so much more to offer
than what we currently give.
something beautiful, something pure.

I believe in giving
the benefit of the doubt.
because love is all around,
always out and about.

and I wonder when (because it's not an if)
we will all learn
how to love every beautiful thing,
including ourselves.

samantha tellez

I always feel alienated
being Mexican-American.
I'm on both sides of a battle
but, I can never win.

I'm not one
and I'm not the other.
I'm kin to all,
but no one's sister or brother.

I'm half loved and half despised
on both sides.
they all want to hear my laughs,
but never my cries.

when I call for help,
not one will respond.
but when I claim either land
they'll go above and beyond
to reassure me
that I am a visitor
and not a tenant.

to whom it may concern

you can dab away
and clean the spill.
but you can't get back
the man you killed.
you can utter a thousand apologies
and swear that you meant no harm
but you can't turn back
and put down the arm.

- *napkin: on police brutality*

samantha tellez

your green eyes signaled me to go forth
and the beautiful traces of yellow in them
warned me to slow down.
the shade of pink on your lips,
so dark that it could pass for red,
made me slam on my brakes
but I already knew,
it was too late for me to turn back.

to whom it may concern

in response to every life lesson I have ever learned from my mother, part 1 of 3

"don't say it if you don't mean it"
I told him that I no longer wanted to be with him because he was hurting me too much. but I didn't want him to leave, I never did.

"be careful of what you wish for, it may come true"
I wished him away and now all I wish for is his return. does it work that way?

"if you love someone, make sure they know"
not a full 24 hours went by in the 438 days we were together in which I didn't remind him that I truly believed my heart was crafted to love his. he knew. he knows. but what good is that now?

"crying isn't going to solve anything"
I know that crying a river isn't going to change anything but that's all I know how to do right now.

"learn from your mistakes"
all I've learned from his departure is that I can't live with it.

in response to every life lesson I have ever learned from my mother, part 2 of 3

"some things are better left unsaid"
I learned that the day I begged for him to come back to me. it fed his ego, but it left me hollow.

"everything happens for a reason"
what escapes me is how this could have been in someone's plan. to love, then leave.

"there's always someone who loves more"
I'm starting to think I was the only one who ever loved at all.

"if it makes you happy, hold on to it"
he left.

"there's a time and a place for everything"
is there ever a time for a broken heart? is there ever a place for a broken heart? it seems that there's only a time and a place for the heartbreaker.

in response to every life lesson I have ever learned from my mother, part 3 of 3

"everyone deserves a second chance"
from time to time, I wake up at the oddest, earliest hours and wonder if some people just don't deserve more if you already gave them everything. I don't think he does.

"it's never too late to apologize"
maybe. but that doesn't mean that he'll mean it.

"time heals everything"
but that's how it ended. he decided that he needed time to himself. how could the same thing that broke me, heal me?

"don't take everything to heart"
I don't want to. but that's just where he is.

"true love only comes once in a lifetime"
does it ever come back?

your lips were so warm, but your heart was so cold and I wondered what lied in-between.

to whom it may concern

tonight,
I'll kiss you.
tomorrow,
I'll miss you.
a week from now,
you'll carry on.
a couple of days down,
I still won't move on.

samantha tellez

I could meet someone new
and forget your face.
but at the end of the day,
you could never be replaced.

to whom it may concern

I have read you like a novel.
I have flipped every page,
and folded the corners of my favorite parts.
I have read in-between the lines,
I have analyzed every word,
and I have sounded out every syllable.
I have read and reread,
I have looked back time after time,
and still, I have yet to find a happy ending for us.

samantha tellez

I miss hearing those three words fall from your lips and into my heart,
but for now, that one word is more than enough.

-   *hello*

to whom it may concern

I love you,
and I wish you loved me, too.
but you do not know,
and I will not let you.

samantha tellez

you are the snow that freezes the thought of you into my mind.

you are the rain that drowns me in your love.

you are the beams that burn your memory into the back of my mind.

you are the breeze that pushes me back to you time after time.

to whom it may concern

if I had my life flash before my eyes, I'd see you.

samantha tellez

there's no sense
in me damning you to hell,
when I still pray to God
that you're doing well.

it'd be foolish
for me to say that I wish we would've
never became more than friends
when if I had the chance,
I'd do the same thing all over again.

when I run into someone from back home, it's the first thing I'm asked. when I meet up with my friends for brunch, it's the first thing they bring up. when I call up my family, they ask about us before they ask about me. and in the awkward silence that lingers in the moments while I'm scrambling to find the words to say that you ceased to be mine a month ago, I find you. and unlike that silence, the silence I find in the thought of you brings me nothing but peace. ever since you left, I have only ever found you quietly. I find you in every hushed moment of my turbulent life. because that's what you were. a sweet lullaby in the midst of havoc. and that's what you will always be.

samantha tellez

maybe we're magnets
and no matter how far apart we grow,
whenever we're near each other
we'll always connect.

to whom it may concern

I'm not a morning person
but waking up next to you
became the best part of all my days.

I'm not a morning person
but having you be the first thing I see every day
has made the first moments of the day more than tolerable.

I'm not a morning person
but kissing you in the early hours
gave me something to smile about for the rest of the day.

I'm not a morning person
but loving you
has made me love every hour of every day.

samantha tellez

breathe;
look around, you'll be fine.
let these thoughts escape your mind.

inhale;
take it in,
this is a battle you're bound to win.

exhale;
let it all out.
give it time, it will pass.

pain never lasts.

-    survivor: for my mother

to whom it may concern

imagine a world
with no yellow, red, or blue.
oh, how the world would be a better place
if that statement was true.

imagine a world
with no preset thought of hate.
perhaps the world would learn to love
if we could live in such a cordial state.

imagine a world
diagnosed with color blindness.
our hue would no longer speak for us,
and our significance would never again be second-guessed.

samantha tellez

there will be days
in which you have no interest
in waking up.
the sun's rays and
the bird's chirps
will not be enough to get you out of bed.
the pound of the alarm
will do nothing but remind you
of all the danger in the world.
the morning news
will only remind you of how cruel
the people of this world can be.
the caffeine in your daily brew
will only give you enough energy to wipe your eyes
and stare at the ceiling.
and on those days
I can only hope and pray
that I will be enough.

to whom it may concern

even after all these years,
it still feels new.
it's you,
always gonna be you.

samantha tellez

I can learn to live without you, but don't mistake that for moving on.

to whom it may concern

tossing and turning,
where are you now?
breaking and yearning,
I can't live without you, teach me how.

samantha tellez

*you're twenty-one when you leave a nightclub after the second song plays
because the man buying you a drink held your hand like he used to.*

*you're twenty-three when you run out of a job interview because the man
behind the desk has brown eyes that look too much like his.*

*you're twenty-five when you excuse yourself to use the restroom in the
middle of a date and never return because his laugh sounds a lot like his
once did.*

*you're twenty-seven when you say "no" to a man who asks you to dance at
your best friend's wedding because this is the song he used to love.*

*you're twenty-nine when you give up on love completely because you're
looking for him in every man you meet.*

-   if you don't move on now, you never will

to whom it may concern

I've never been good
at moving on.
all I ever knew
was how to hold on.
I'll flip through old photographs
and listen to our song.
some nights, I'll even sleep with your sweater and
believe me, I know it's wrong,
but I've never been good
at moving on.

samantha tellez

just because I stopped
thinking about you,
it doesn't mean that I never
think about you at all.

I may have stopped
wanting you,
but it's not that easy
to undo the fall.

and although I no longer
have the same love for you,
that doesn't mean that
when I see your face, I don't recall.

to whom it may concern

and although we have touched
a thousand times before,
you make me feel things
I've never felt before.

samantha tellez

living without you
is a lot like
riding a bike
without training wheels.
I don't think I can
until I have no choice but to.
this is the only time
I'll thank you
for forcing something onto me.

to whom it may concern

I hope
one day
you stop
feeling guilty
about being
human.

samantha tellez

LOVING

to whom it may concern

love is not perfect,
but to love you is.

samantha tellez

I want the awkward linking
of two pairs of lips that
have never kissed anyone
but their mothers before.

I want the awkward smile
you give each other
when you walk past
each other with your friends.

I want the awkward embrace
that always seems to happen
in front of our parents
when it's time for you to go.

I want the awkward love
of a young pair,
simply because you and I
experienced it with different people.

to love someone means a world of things. sometimes, it means holding the door for you even when I'm already running five minutes late. sometimes, it means staying in on a summer night because you somehow managed to catch a cold in 80 degree weather. sometimes, it means driving with the windows down even though I just got my hair done because music sounds better that way. sometimes, it means you praying a rosary with me even though you're an atheist. sometimes, it means you paying the extra dollar for cream and sugar because I like it better that way. sometimes, it means you joining me on my run even though you'd rather walk. and for us, sometimes, it means growing apart so that we may grow together.

samantha tellez

the love I have for you
could never be matched.
not in quantity,
nor in quality.

to whom it may concern

in your eyes
I saw the only love
I'd ever want to see.

the very love
I'd like to see
first thing every morning.

the very love I'd like to see
across my dining room table
every Saturday night.

the very love
I'd like to see
curled up beside me on stormy nights.

the very love
I'd like to see;
but he's the very love
that can't even bring himself
to make eye contact with me.

samantha tellez

you are the type of person
people spend their whole lives looking for.
and I have yet to meet someone
quite like you before.

I know how to love,
but not someone like you.
you are too pure, too beautiful,
almost too good to be true.

I am in constant fear
of ruining you.
I wish you were
too good to be true.

to whom it may concern

I found a string of prose latched in-between the thinnest layers of skin coating your top and bottom lip. poems spilled out of them every time you opened your mouth like spoken word screaming to be heard. rhymes simply floated out of your being every time your lips parted. you were poetry. and you were the best I ever read.

samantha tellez

ever since the day we met, all I knew,
was that I wanted to run away with you.

somewhere far from where we are,
where we can lay and watch the stars.

cheap motels, aimless car rides,
not having a clue where we're going, letting the road decide.

becoming strangers to someone's hometown,
pick a place, and we'll settle down.

for you, I'd travel all over the nation,
regardless of our final destination.

to whom it may concern

he said, "the problem with love today
is that they tell you
to be with someone you love,
but they never tell you
to be with someone who loves you".

I said, "no, the problem with love today
is that they tell you
to be with someone you love,
but they never tell you
to be someone you love".

- self-love is love, too

my heart does not know you,
but my heart does know that it loves you.

my mind knows little of you,
but my mind is flooded with thoughts of you.

my soul hasn't met yours,
but my soul is meant for yours.

my body hasn't felt yours,
but my body feels your absence.

I love you,
but haven't really had the chance to yet.

pet name, part 1 of 3

you're my baby. I do not mean for that to be interpreted in the sense of a cliché, so do not take it that way. what I mean is that you are my baby. something I want to look after for as long as I live. something that I feel I must nurture and take care of. something that I want to grow with. something that I want to hold onto forever. something so pure and innocent that I never wish to be corrupted. something I want everyone to know is mine. you're my baby.

pet name, part 2 of 3

you're my love. I do not mean for that to be interpreted in the sense of a cliché, so do not take it that way. what I mean is that you are my love. you are what I adore. you are what I care for. you are what I have dreamed of night after night. you are all I need. you are what gets me through the day. you are the only thing that doesn't hurt. you are the only thing that will ever matter. you are what I feel for you. you're my love.

pet name, part 3 of 3

you're my darling. I do not mean for that to be interpreted in the sense of a cliché, so do not take it that way. what I mean is that you are my darling. you are the most beautiful thing in the room. you are what I want to show off at every party. you are what catches everyone's eye. you are the thing that even in its simplest form will outshine all else. you are what everyone wants, but few will ever have. you're my darling.

samantha tellez

we were always
better off as strangers.
it's a shame I only knew
after loving you.

to whom it may concern

no longer
do you attempt to mask
how your longing for me
only exists externally.

I could kiss
every inch of your skin,
but never could I
kiss your heart.

you have stripped me
to flesh and bone.
this is all you see,
and so, this is all I will ever be.

because I can make love
to you
but I cannot
make you love me.

samantha tellez

"remember to put me first this time" my heart whispered to me before I opened the door for you.

to whom it may concern

part of me
will always love you.
right now,
all of me loves you.

I don't know
what to make of this.
I have many pieces of you left,
but not the ones that I miss.

I feel like you're asking me to stay,
but to leave the door open.
I can spend the night,
but if someone knocks, I must let them in.

samantha tellez

action speaks louder than word,
and as we are
your love is the sweetest sound
I've ever heard.

and one day, "meet me halfway" no longer meant where River Street and Bridge Avenue crossed: half a mile from your house and half a mile from mine. but, "come to my soccer game even though you hate the sport", "try this Sashimi even though the smell of seafood makes your stomach queasy", "watch this movie even though we've seen it several times before just because it's my favorite", "talk it out with me even though it's the last thing you want to do right now" and most importantly, "love me even when you don't want to".

samantha tellez

you are loved by everyone,
and I have never wanted to fit in so badly.

to whom it may concern

I crave a new love,
a love that won't let me down.
if such a love exists,
I pray that it will come around.

                              I crave a new love,
                  a love that is genuine and true.
                              if such a love exists,
                  I want it to be for us two.

I crave a new love,
a love that will take me over the moon.
if such a love exists,
I would love for it to come soon.

                              I crave a new love,
                  a love that will always pull through.
                              if such a love exists,
                  I hope that it resides in you.

samantha tellez

I want you to know
that you're all I think about.
most of my feelings come and go,
but you're the only thing I don't doubt.

I think I need you,
in a way I have never needed before.
I need you the way I love you,
or maybe even more.

to whom it may concern

our lips have never touched, but every now and then, you'd smile back at me and that was always enough. your hands never held mine, but sometimes they would brush over my skin, and to me, that was always enough. your arms never wrapped around me in an embrace but you always said the sweetest words, and that was always enough. you never said you loved me, but I knew you did, somewhere deep down inside of you. and to me, that was always enough.

samantha tellez

I have convinced myself
that you and I
are from the same galaxy.
the same stars that crafted you,
crafted me.
and so, when we love,
love all that can
and love to our demise,
you and I
we will return to stardust,
we will return to the skies,
together, again.

to whom it may concern

you wrote me love letters
disguised as haikus
and mixtapes.
for if there were
no real trace,
my love and justification for it
had no case.
never could I match
the name "love"
to your beautiful face.

do not treat me like a stray in your hotel room heart. rather, treat me like a guest in your childhood bedroom. expose me to all of the things you never wanted me to see, all of the things you have always dreamed of sharing, and all of the things you never thought you'd allow for anyone else to see. hold the door open for me on my way in and allow me to unpack my bags even if I'm only staying for the night. give me your blessing to make myself right at home, in yours. do not treat me like a stray in your hotel room heart. because I am not a visitor.

to whom it may concern

you love me in the summer,
only when I'm ripened.
every other season
you only wish to be a friend.

you love me solely at my finest
like I don't exist until I've peaked.
it's only at my best
that you pick me.

samantha tellez

you came knocking on my door seconds after the clock declared it was a quarter past eleven. you said you needed a place to stay, muttering something about being kicked out of your girlfriend's house. and with open arms, I welcomed you. I did not offer you the guest bedroom. instead, I offered you an air mattress adjacent to my bed. you laid awake for approximately an hour, flooding me with words of thanks and reassurance that you would be out soon; before I knew it. all I did was smile and say that you could stay for as long as you needed; as long as you wanted. and as you dozed off into a deep slumber, I stayed up. weeks later, you packed your things and moved in with your oldest brother and his fiancée. yet, even long after the fact, you failed to recognize that when she let you out, it wasn't simply out of her house. and that when I let you in, it wasn't simply into my quaint apartment.

to whom it may concern

I loved you
as a seed.
when you didn't have wants,
but rather, needs.

I loved you
as a sprout.
when you were neither in,
nor were you out.

I love you
as a plant.
when I want to contribute to your growth,
but can't.

samantha tellez

I think you're the most
beautiful person I've ever met.
I do not say that lightly,
so do not take it that way.

I have loved a thousand times,
but to love like this, I have yet.

to whom it may concern

I love you. not solely in the sense that I care for you, nor solely in the sense that I adore you. I love you in a "pretend I'm not hungry so you can have the last slice of pizza" type of way. I love you in an "I'll laugh at your jokes even when they're not that funny so that you don't feel embarrassed" type of way. I love you in an "I'm going to check your horoscope because you said you're okay but I just want to be sure" type of way. I love you in an "I'm praying for you tonight even though you don't believe in God" type of way. I love you in an "I'm letting you change the station even though this song is really good because I know you hate country music" type of way. I love you in an "I want you to pick what movie we're watching even though my favorite show is on" type of way. I love you in an "I want you to finish your sentence even though I could argue the first thing that came out of your mouth" type of way. I love you. not solely in the sense that I care for you, nor solely in the sense that I adore you.

samantha tellez

every now and then
I ponder upon the question
"is love real?"

every now and then
I look to you
and smiling, I think,
"how could it not be?"

to whom it may concern

I'm in love with your happiness.
and the way you stick your tongue out when you run,
and the way your nose crinkles when you laugh too hard,
and the way your voice cracks when you're talking too fast,
and the way your eyes twitch when it's too early for them to open,
and the way you tap your fingers when you can't focus,
and the way you treat people like you have never been broken,
but maybe they have,
and the way you hold me as if I might break if you let go
and the way I could fill an entire damn page with things I love about
you.

samantha tellez

and they'll say that there's no point,
if I can't always hear your voice,
but what they don't understand,
is that falling for you wasn't a choice.

although it kills me to know that I can't
always see your smile
knowing that you love me back,
makes it all worthwhile.

you're my entire world,
even when we aren't face-to-face.
you're my entire world,
and you could never be replaced.

to whom it may concern

it doesn't sound as sweet
when I call our love
inconsistent
rather than unpredictable.

when I no longer
guard what I think we have
from what we truly have,
everything shifts.

samantha tellez

"let's just be casual" he suggests.

but how could I just be casual with someone who makes me feel the way sunshine on my shoulders does? how could I just be casual with someone who when I hear their name, my heart smiles? how could I just be casual with someone whose voice plays over and over in my head like a melody I hope I never forget? how could I just be casual with someone whose eyes have replaced Manhattan's skyline as my favorite view? how could I just be casual with someone who I lay awake at night dreaming of a future with? how could I just be casual with someone I pray for, even though I'm not really sure I believe in anything but him? how?

"sure" I replied.

to whom it may concern

I hate you the way I hate
running long distance
(which always left me feeling breathless,
something you always did)

I hate you the way I hate
throwing up
(which always left me feeling empty,
something you always did)

I hate you the way I hate
the smell of alcohol
(which always left me feeling anxious,
something you always did)

I hate you the way I hate
the fact that I still love you
(which always left me feeling foolish,
something you still do)

I'll sneak you into my room in the depths of the night
and whisper, "don't make any noise".
I'll lock the door, turn off every light,
and silently say, "watch your step".
I'll tiptoe across the floor in fright
and still beg, "please be careful".
hours will pass and you'll think we're alright.
because we haven't been caught
and there's not another soul in sight.
but, what you don't know
is that when I said to be careful,
I was talking about my heart.

to whom it may concern

you only cared when I was sprawled out on your stained bedsheets,
and you only ever bothered when you caressed my skin
or raised my heartbeat.

you only remembered my name when I was screaming yours,
and you were only ever sure
when my clothes were on your bedroom floor.

you only loved me when the springs in your mattress squeaked,
and I knew you never really did when just moments later,
I'd hear you tiptoe across the hardwood
and listen to the floor creak.

I wonder what you tell your friends about me. maybe you tell them that I taste sweeter than the last nameless girl they saw you guide upstairs (they have no way of knowing how bitter you have made me). maybe you tell them that I feel amazing (they have no way of knowing how awful I always feel leaving your place). maybe you tell them that it's the best you have ever had (they have no way of knowing that you have made me feel the worst I have ever felt about myself). maybe you tell them that I would let you do whatever you wanted to me (they have no way of knowing that you are taking advantage of this). maybe you tell them that I'm a little clingy (they have no way of knowing that it's because I'm losing pieces of myself to you). maybe you tell them that you have me wrapped around your finger (they have no way of knowing that I'm really just totally, and completely in love with you).

to whom it may concern

I see you
ever so clearly,
and love you
ever so dearly.
but it's like
there's glass in-between
you and I.
I can look,
but I can't touch,
and to ask for more
would be too much.

samantha tellez

it hurts to love you
knowing that friends is all we'll ever be.
because baby, I'd love you
even if you hated me.

to whom it may concern

please,
come home.
I'll do all the laundry,
because I know you don't know the difference
between detergent and softener.
I'll cook all three meals,
because I know that otherwise,
you'll live off of take-out.
I'll do all the cleaning,
because I know how
dust makes you sneeze nonstop.
and I'll even do all the loving,
because I know that's
too much to ask from you.
and I'll even do all the loving,
because I know
you won't.

samantha tellez

telling you how I felt was the most liberating, yet constricting thing I
had ever done. it got my words out, but in a sense, I felt that it bound
me to them. as if to feel anything other than verbatim what I said,
would be to betray them and of course, you. I feel stuck in love.

to whom it may concern

your smile shines brighter
than all of the stars I wish upon to see it again.

samantha tellez

*the words we say to each other past ten p.m. are like torn pieces of
notebook paper being passed through a classroom in a secondary
school. sweet. innocent. pure. every time our lips part, another secret
escapes like an adolescent charging towards the blacktop at the cue of
the fifth bell. anxious. hopeful. eager. soon, you will not have the words
to satisfy my inquiries and we will simply stare at each other like an
instructor at their scholars in silence. desperate. exasperated. agitated.
in the end, you will grow out of this phase and halt all feelings you ever
had for me. and then I'll be left alone like a child who was just scolded
for something that they didn't do but took the blame for anyway.*

to whom it may concern

you'll fall for the man
sitting alone on a stool at a bar.
you'll ask if the seat beside his is taken.
he'll say no, and offer you a puff of his cigar.

you don't smoke, so you'll politely decline,
but you'll accept a drink when offered.
he'll make you smile,
and tell you that your laugh is the most beautiful thing he's ever heard.

one thing will lead to another,
and you'll learn to trust him.
he'll tell you about his past,
and you'll finally understand why his glass is always filled to the brim.

you'll learn to love him,
and he'll learn to love you.
he'll soon tell you about his other addiction,
but this one's new.

he'll put aside the glass and the cigarettes,
yet will continue his life as an addict.
his past addictions chose him,
but this one was handpicked.

samantha tellez

he color coded his meal
but told me that he loved
both the green and the brown
in my eyes.

- how I knew he loved me

to whom it may concern

love is when someone asks about your day
and always says goodnight.
love is when someone holds the door for you
and makes sure you're alright.

love is when someone tells you that you look great
and checks if you have your seatbelt on.
love is when someone holds your hand
and remembers your favorite song.

love is when someone kisses your forehead
and offers you a sip.
love is when someone laughs at your jokes
and wishes you a safe trip.

love is when someone reminds you of your worth
and makes you smile.
love is when someone can talk to you for hours
and makes it all worthwhile.

samantha tellez

a week ago you said to me, "do you believe in love?"

and between the split seconds those five words escaped your lips, I thought of you and all of the times you proved love to be more than a word. for every time you made me tilt my head back in laughter, and for all of the times you made me feel like I had won the lottery. for every time you made me smile until the apples of my cheeks hurt and for every time I stayed up thinking about how lucky I was to have you. for every time you made me wonder what I did to deserve someone like you, and for every time you made all the cheesy love songs make sense. for every time you made me feel beautiful, and for every time you left me completely and utterly breathless. for every time you gave me butterflies and for every time I asked myself if you just might be the one.

a week ago you said to me, "do you believe in love?"
and I said, "yes, yes I do"

to whom it may concern

I hope you fall in love
with someone who thinks your eyes are brighter
than all of the stars in the sky.

I hope you fall in love
with someone who thinks your laugh is more euphonious
than their favorite soundtrack.

I hope you fall in love
with someone who thinks your smile alone is prettier
than any soul they have ever met.

but most of all,
I hope you fall in love
with someone who treats you better
than you treated me.

samantha tellez

I want you and I,
just us two.
all I need
is for you to want me, too.

the two of us,
so free and content.
all I need
is your consent.

to whom it may concern

watching you throw your head back in laughter,
or not being able to help a smirk from forming over a dumb joke.
watching your eyes squint as the result of a smile,
or hearing a joke and seeing you're the only one laughing minutes after.

seeing your eyes light up at the mention of something you enjoy,
or witnessing a grin forming upon hearing your favorite song.
regardless of what causes it,
seeing you happy brings me utmost joy.

I'm in love with your happiness,
and I think that's what love is.
being happy because you are,
and I get to be your witness.

samantha tellez

I'd say it's a privilege to know you,
even if it's not as well as I'd like to.

> I'd say it's a privilege to hold you,
> even if it's not as close as I'd like to.

I'd say it's a privilege to love you,
even if it's not the way I'd like to.

> would you say the same?

to whom it may concern

one day,
you will come across someone
that there are no words for.
they will be unlike anyone
you have ever met before.

when you find this person,
hold on tight.

to let them go would be a sin.

samantha tellez

maybe I knew you in a different life. perhaps that is why the curves on your palms line up so perfectly with mine. why your laugh sounds like a melody I once heard on the radio but I, for the life of me, cannot remember the name of. why your eyes reflect sunsets I have never seen, cities I have never visited, and days I have never lived. why your kiss tastes of delicacies that have never touched my lips but I feel I'll crave for the rest of my life. why the things you say resonate within me like a profound quote I read in a magazine once but cannot cite. why the way you held me never gave me rigors, like my skin was sewn together to be held against yours and for that only. why I have missed you before I had even met you. maybe that's why I never felt that your love simply came to me, but rather that it came back to me.

to whom it may concern

when we first met
you were over twenty;
allowed to drink at every pub.
I wasn't old enough
to even enter a nightclub.

you weren't old enough
to be a guardian,
and not quite young enough
to be just a friend.

we always had something to hide.
and when it came to your feelings,
you could never decide.

soon, you pushed my love to the side.
you said maybe we'd meet again,
when we're older,
and don't have anything to hide.

every second we're getting older,
and every second we have less to hide.
why haven't we spent a single second since
by each other's side?

samantha tellez

it's funny
how you
describe us
as having
"no strings attached"
as if
you do not
pull my strings
and control
my every movement

-    puppet love

to whom it may concern

I'm not very religious
but every time we lock eyes
you prove to me
that heaven does exist.

samantha tellez

you say
"there's just no way
it could ever work"
in your string of justifications
as if you
have never met love.

love would always
make it work.

to whom it may concern

about the book

Greg Kinnear's character in my favorite movie, stuck in love, said: "a writer is the sum of his experiences, go get some". I have always liked to think of my work as an extension of who I am, and so, simply put, "to whom it may concern" is the sum of my experiences. it's organized by four verbs I feel capture my eighteen years of life best, and categorizing my pieces in this manner is something that means a lot to me. at first, I thought to categorize by years, as any piece in this book could have been written when I was 12, or 17. then, by the seen and unseen, as any piece could have been uploaded online before and seen by thousands, or torn straight from my journal, only seen by myself. but, after attempting both, I found that those factors did not mean as much to me as knowing that there was a human experience attached to my work did. the learning, leaving, living and loving are what meant the most to me. reiterating that what you are reading is not a figment of my imagination, but a fragment of my reality is so important to me. you hold the sum of my experiences.

to whom it may concern

about the author

my name is Samantha Tellez. I'm from a small town you've likely never heard of in Pennsylvania and I have lived here for the past 18 years that my heart's been beating. come fall, I'll be attending West Chester University to study business management. to keep up with my work, visit Instagram.com/stpoems

samantha tellez

Made in the USA
Middletown, DE
29 November 2021

53725409R00113